NEAT SIDE EDGES

NEAT SIDE EDGES

Simple Ways
to Keep the Edges
of Your Knitted Projects
Nice and Tidy

Maryna Shevchenko

10 Rows a Day

ISBN 978-1-7386402-0-1 paperback
ISBN 978-1-7386402-1-8 e-book

Cover design by:
Sasha Shevchenko
www.sasha-shevchenko.com

Published in Canada

To everyone
who finds joy in knitting

CONTENTS

INTRODUCTION

When we want to improve the side edges of a project, we should remember to work side stitches in a way that guarantees that the edges are uniform and nice-looking. These important stitches have a special name – selvedges.

There are a number of ways to work selvedge stitches with each way creating a different look. In this book, we'll discuss twelve of those ways – four methods that form neat edges one-stitch wide, four methods that are worked over two selvedge stitches at each side of the work, and four ways to make gorgeous wide side edges.

We'll also talk about fixing dropped edge stitches in stockinette and garter stitch fabric, and I'll show you a way to make any side edge neater after the project is finished.

It doesn't matter whether you hold yarn in your left or in your right hand. These edgings work well with any classic knitting style.

To provide a quick reference, I made quick reference cards with concise step-by-step photo instructions that illustrate each method explained in this book. Feel free to cut these pages out of the book to keep them at hand in your knitting bag.

It is always more fun to learn new knitting techniques together with other knitters. At the very end of the book, I suggest a few ways to use this book in knitting groups and other knitting communities.

I hope these methods and tips will help you to make the edges of your projects neat and clean.

Happy knitting, my friend!

Maryna

ONE-STITCH EDGES

Slip-Stitch Selvedges

Silesian Selvedges

Slip-Stitch Knotted Edge

Garter Stitch Selvedges

These edges are formed by one stitch at each side edge of the fabric.

When using these methods, **add two stitches to the number of stitches you cast on** – one stitch for each side of the project.

SLIP-STITCH SELVEDGES

We'll start by taking a look at the easiest way to make neat side edges. This method is very popular and there is a reason for that – this way to work selvedges has a simple one-row repeat that is easy to remember.

The edge formed by this variation of slip-stitch selvedges looks like a **chain of slightly elongated stitches**. These edges are **stretchy** enough not to jam the fabric, and they work great with **any stitch pattern**.

SETUP

To make this type of selvedges, cast on **two extra stitches**. For example, if your pattern tells you to cast on 50 stitches, cast on 52.

Then **slip the first stitch and purl the last stitch of every row**. Here's how we do it **step by step**:

STEP 1

With the yarn at the back of the work, slip the first stitch **purlwise** from the left needle to the right needle (insert the right needle into the stitch **from right to left**).

STEP 2

Work all stitches in the pattern of your choice until you get **to the last stitch** of the row.

STEP 3

Purl the last stitch.

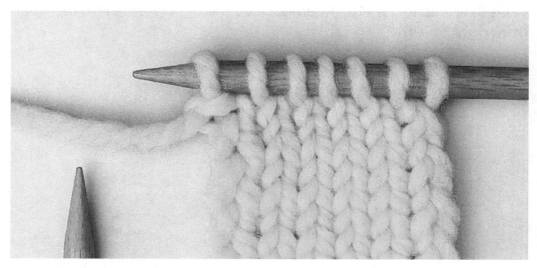

Repeat these steps in **every row** (both right side and wrong side), and you'll make a beautiful chain of stitches at each side of the work.

If the chain of stitches is **too loose** and you want to fix it, **pull the yarn a bit** after you work the second stitch of every row.

Each "link" of the chain is created **every two rows**. That's handy when we need to **count the rows**. Simply count the links of the chain and **double that number**.

SILESIAN SELVEDGES

The method described in this tutorial is also based on slipping edge stitches, but in a slightly different way.

I learned this **simple yet effective** method from Friederike – a knitter in our virtual knitting community. She kindly shared with me a way that **her mother used** to make edges of her projects neat and tidy. I tested this technique and instantly fell in love with it.

This type of selvedges forms a **chain of twisted stitches** at each side of the fabric. The chains look very similar to the ones formed by Slip-Stitch Selvedges method (page 10), but they seem to be **neater** and **don't stretch as much**.

I don't know the formal name for this method, but because Friederike's Mom comes from a region in Central Europe called Silesia, I called this technique **Silesian Selvedges**.

Let's see how we can make these lovely edges in **three simple steps**.

SETUP

If you decide to treat the edges of your project with Silesian selvedges, **add two stitches** to the total number of stitches you cast on – one stitch for each side edge of the fabric. Then work the steps explained below **starting from the very first row**.

STEP 1

Knit the first stitch **through the back loop.** To do that, insert the right needle **from right to left** into the first stitch on the left needle.

Wrap the tip of the right needle with the yarn, and pull the wrap through to form a new stitch.

STEP 2

Work in the pattern of your choice until you get **to the last stitch** of the row.

One of the best things about this technique is that it works with **the majority of stitch patterns**. Whenever you want to trim the sides of your project with a lovely slim edging, add Silesian selvedges no matter what stitch pattern you use as the main pattern of your project.

STEP 3

Bring the yarn **to the front of the work,** and slip the last stitch of the row **purlwise**. That means inserting the right needle into the stitch **from right to left**, just as we did in step 1.

That's how simple it is. **Repeat these three steps in every row** and you will see that each side edge of your project turns into a pretty chain making the piece look neat and well-finished.

SLIP-STITCH KNOTTED EDGE

This is a go-to way to make selvedge stitches when you are after a fairly rigid edge that resembles a string of beads.

The knotted edge formed by this method holds shape well and doesn't create loopy edges. It is **not as stretchy** as the Slip-Stitch Selvedges (page 10). Rather, it has **about the same elasticity** as the edge formed by the Silesian Selvedges (page 13).

Even though this edging looks very different from the edging created by the Slip-Stitch Selvedges, both types of selvedges are **formed in a similar way**. The only difference between these methods is that we **knit the last stitch** (instead of purling it) when we use the Slip-Stitch Knotted Edge method.

It's incredible that such a **small difference** can drastically **change the look** and the feel of the edging.

SETUP

To make this type of selvedges, **add two stitches** to the number of stitches you cast on.

Then **slip the first stitch and knit the last stitch of every row**. Here's how we do it **step by step**.

STEP 1

With the **yarn at the back of the work**, slip the first stitch **purlwise** from the left needle to the right needle.

That means that we should insert the right needle into the stitch **from right to left**, and then ease the left needle out, leaving the stitch on the right needle.

Starting with the second row, the first stitch will look like a purl, and it might **seem natural** to keep the yarn at the front of the work before we slip the first stitch. Don't give in to that feeling! It is **very important** to bring the yarn to the **back of the work** before you slip the first stitch.

Otherwise, the edge will look **more like a chain of stitches** and it will not get decorated with the cute little knots that make this selvedge method so appealing.

STEP 2

Work all stitches in the pattern of your choice until you get **to the last stitch**.

STEP 3

Knit the last stitch.

Repeat these steps **in every row** and watch the edges of your project turn into a string of tiny bead-like knots.

You can create a **similar look** if you **knit the first and the last stitches** of every row. This method is called the Garter Stitch Selvedges. It is a good way to add a special treatment to the edges of a project, but the **edge will be more elastic**.

The good thing about the Slip-Stitch Knotted Edge is that it **doesn't stretch as much as garter stitch**. That makes it a slightly better-looking option.

But if you want to make an edge **with more elasticity** without sacrificing the knotted look of the selvedges, **keep reading on** to the next chapter.

GARTER STITCH SELVEDGES

As it is implied by the name, this type of edging is formed by one-stitch vertical stripes worked in garter stitch.

By adding one garter stitch at each side of the work, we take advantage both of the **lovely bead-like look** of this stitch pattern and of its **tendency to stay flat**.

It is also **one of the easiest ways** to make the side edges of our projects neater. This method is so easy that even an absolute beginner knitter will be able to add these selvedges to their projects.

All we have to do is **knit the first and the last stitch** of every row.

Here's how we do it **step by step**.

SETUP

Add two stitches to the number of stitches you cast on – one extra stitch for each side edge of your project.

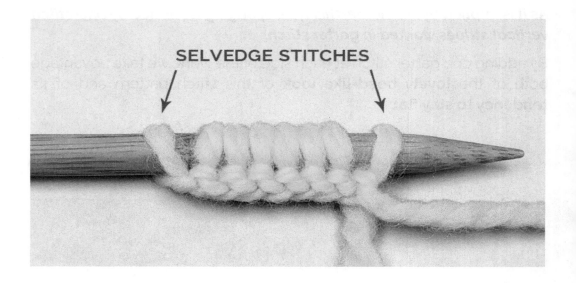

SELVEDGE STITCHES

STEP 1

Knit 1 stitch.

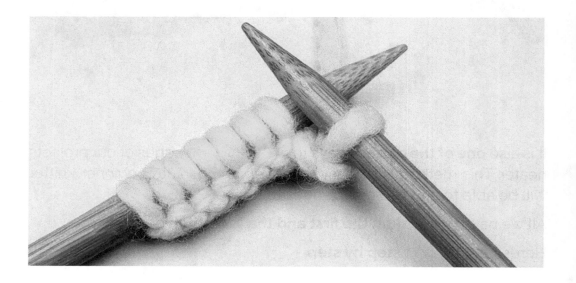

STEP 2

Work in the main stitch pattern until you get **to the last stitch**.

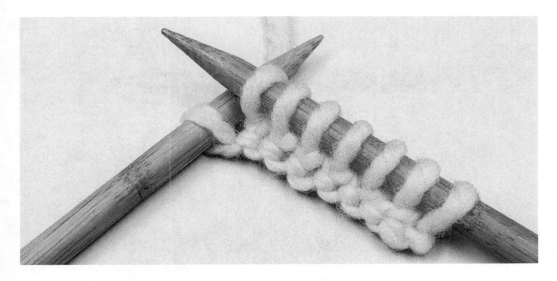

My swatch is made in stockinette stitch, so I knitted all stitches until I got to the last stitch of the row.

STEP 3

Knit the last stitch.

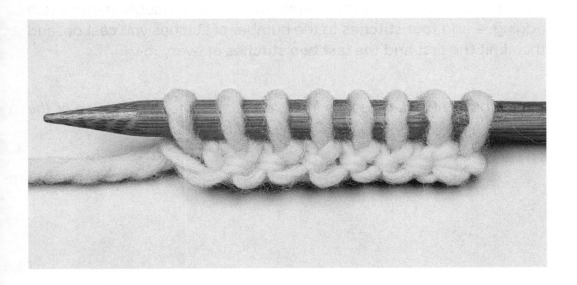

Repeat these three steps **in every row** and you will form a lovely non-curling edge that **looks like a string of beads** on both sides of the fabric.

To add this edging **only to the right edge** of the fabric, knit the first stitch in one row and knit the last stitch in the next row.

If you want to use this edging **only at the left edge** of your project, knit the last stitch in one row and knit the first stitch in the next row.

For a **more prominent garter stitch look**, make a double garter stitch edging — add **four stitches** to the number of stitches you cast on, and then **knit the first and the last two stitches** of every row.

We'll explore two-stitch edges in more detail in the next section of the book.

SLIP-STITCH CHAIN EDGE

Add **two stitches** to the number of stitches you cast on.

With the yarn at the back of the work, slip the first stitch purlwise from the left needle to the right needle.

Work in the main stitch pattern to the end of the row.

Purl the last stitch.

Repeat these steps in every row (both right side and wrong side).

Quick reference card

SILESIAN SELVEDGES

Add **two stitches** to the number of stitches you cast on.

Knit the first stitch through the back loop.

Work in the main stitch pattern to the last stitch of the row.

Bring the yarn to the front of the work, and slip the last stitch of the row purlwise.

Repeat these steps in every row (both right side and wrong side).

SLIP-STITCH KNOTTED EDGE

Add **two stitches** to the number of stitches you cast on.

With the yarn at the back of the work, slip the first stitch purlwise from the left needle to the right needle

Work in the main stitch pattern to the last stitch of the row.

Knit the last stitch.

Repeat these steps in every row (both right side and wrong side).

Quick reference card

GARTER STITCH SELVEDGES

Add **two stitches** to the number of stitches you cast on.

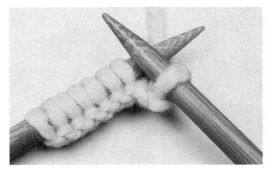

Knit one stitch.

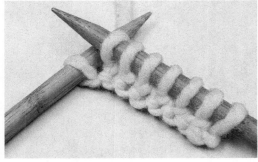

Work in the main stitch pattern to the last stitch of the row.

Knit the last stitch.

Repeat these steps in every row (both right side and wrong side).

TWO-STITCH EDGES

Seed Stitch Edging

Yarn Over Edging

Brioche Selvedges

Slim I-Cord Edging

These edges are formed by two stitches at each side edge of the fabric.

When using these methods, **add four stitches to the number of stitches you cast on** – two stitches for each side of the project.

SEED STITCH EDGING

This method is very similar to the double garter stitch edging mentioned on page 24. The idea is the same — we use a reversible non-curling stitch pattern to make a narrow two-stitch band at each side edge of the work.

Thanks to the balance of knit and purl stitches in the seed stitch pattern, this edging can be used as **a decoration on a delicate project** like lace.

To make this type of edging, cast on the number of stitches required for your project **plus four extra stitches**.

Then **work the first two stitches and the last two stitches of every row in seed stitch** so that the first and the last stitches are knits.

Here's how to do it in **three very simple steps**:

STEP 1

Knit 1 stitch, and then purl 1 stitch.

STEP 2

Work in the pattern of your choice **until you get to the last two stitches** of the row.

STEP 3

This step is the **opposite of the first step** – first, we purl 1 stitch and then we knit 1 stitch.

Repeat these steps **in every row,** and you will form a lovely **fully reversible** edging that keeps the edges of your project **flat and neat**.

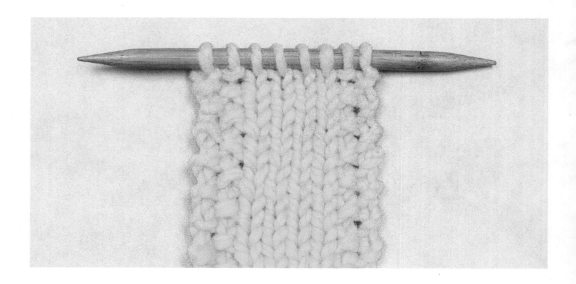

YARN OVER EDGING

There are projects with edges that look like a line of dew drops. We often see them on shawls and scarves, but there is nothing wrong with adding this edging to cardigans, blankets and other projects with open sides.

You **don't need to be an expert** knitter to add these lovely delicate edges to your projects. All you need to do is follow **six simple steps** described in this tutorial.

NOTE

This edging is formed over **two stitches at each side of the work**. If you plan to use this method to decorate both side edges of your project, **add four stitches** to the number of stitches you cast on.

If you are adding this edging to **one side edge** of your project, cast on **two extra stitches**.

To add this edging **only to the right edge of the fabric**, work step 1 in every right-side row and purl the last two stitches of every wrong-side row.

If you plan to decorate **only the left edge of the fabric**, knit the last two stitches in every right-side row, and work step 4 in every wrong-side row.

RIGHT-SIDE ROW

STEP 1

1.1. Make a yarn over.

Adding a yarn over at the beginning of a row could seem **a bit confusing**, but, in fact, it is very simple. **The trick is** to place the right needle **underneath the working yarn** that is hanging at the beginning of the row.

1.2. Make a "slip-slip-knit" (SSK) decrease.

It is perfectly fine to make the **classic SSK decrease**, slipping two stitches one by one knitwise to the right needle, then returning them to the left needle and knitting them together through the back loop, but I prefer to use a **simplified version of this decrease**.

First, insert the tip of the right needle **from left to right** into the first stitch on the left needle and take the left needle out of this stitch **slipping it to the right needle.**

Then, place this stitch **back to the left needle**. This time, do it **purlwise**, without twisting the stitch again. As you do it, **push the tip of the right needle a bit further** so that it enters the next stitch on the left needle.

Finally, wrap the tip of the right needle with the yarn and pull this wrap through **knitting these two stitches together** through the back loop.

No matter whether you choose the classic or the simplified version of this decrease, **make sure you don't lose the yarn over** formed in step 1.1.

STEP 2

Work in a stitch pattern of your choice until you get **to the last two stitches** of the row.

STEP 3

Knit the last two stitches one by one.

WRONG-SIDE ROW

STEP 4

4.1. Make a yarn over.

We already know how to do it. The process is **exactly the same** as the one we used in Step 1 – we simply place the right needle underneath the working yarn.

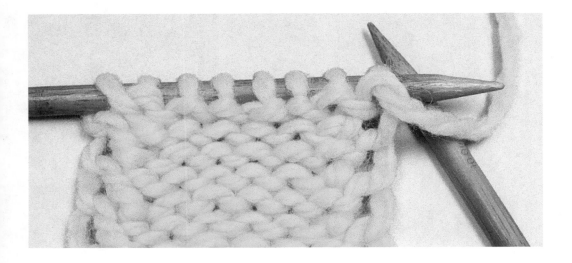

4.2. Purl 2 stitches together.

Remember to **keep an eye on the yarn over** – it should sit on the right needle in front of the stitch that resulted from the decrease.

STEP 5

Work in a stitch pattern of your choice until you get **to the last two stitches**.

STEP 6

Purl the last two stitches one by one.

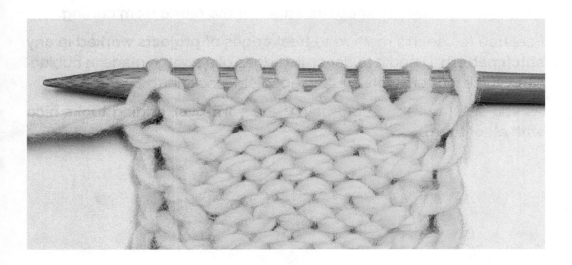

As you **repeat these six steps**, you will see that the edges of your project get embellished by **tiny yarn-over dew drops** accentuated by mirroring slanted stitches formed by decreases.

To open the yarn overs, **stretch and pin each yarn over when you block your project**, or use a piece of blocking wire to make this process faster.

This edging **looks great on both sides of the work**, and the decreases give it enough body to **keep the edges of the fabric from curling.**

Feel free to use this method to treat edges of **projects worked in any stitch pattern**. I used it to decorate edges of a swatch made in ribbing, seed stitch, garter stitch, and the good old stockinette.

As you see from the photo below, the **yarn-over edging looks nice with all of them**.

If you want to make the "dew-drop effect" more prominent, **make each yarn over bigger** in steps 1.1 and 4.1. Or, wrap the yarn around the needle twice to **make a double yarn over,** then unravel one of the wraps in the next row.

BRIOCHE SELVEDGES

Very few knitters don't like the look of the brioche stitch. The rich texture and amazing softness of brioche fabric is the epitome of the cosiness and warmth of hand-knitting.

Even though brioche might not be a good choice for some garments, we can **easily make brioche borders** to add a touch of lusciousness to any project, especially the ones with open side edges like scarves, shawls, blankets and cardigans, because who would want to hide beautiful side edges inside a seam, right?

All we have to do to turn any side edge into a gorgeous fully reversible border is to repeat **two simple steps** in every row as we work on our project.

CAST ON

If the pattern you follow does not include selvedge stitches, **add two stitches to the number of stitches you cast on** — one stitch for each side edge of the project.

When it comes to the type of cast on, feel free to use any one you like. It won't affect the look of the edges.

To make the swatch featured in this tutorial, I cast on stitches using the **long-tail cast on** method.

Even though we are adding one extra stitch to each side of the work, this edging is actually **worked over two stitches** thanks to the yarn overs that we add and then eliminate in every row.

SETUP ROW

Just as it is true for any variation of the brioche stitch pattern, first, we need to work a setup row to give our brioche border a good start. **Here's how we do it:**

Bring the working **yarn to the front** of the work. Then **slip the first stitch purlwise** from the left needle to the right needle.

It means that we insert the tip of the right needle into the first stitch **from right to left**, and then ease the left needle out of that stitch.

Move the working yarn from front to back over the right needle to **make a yarn over**.

Work in a stitch pattern of your choice until you get **to the last stitch** of the row, then knit the last stitch.

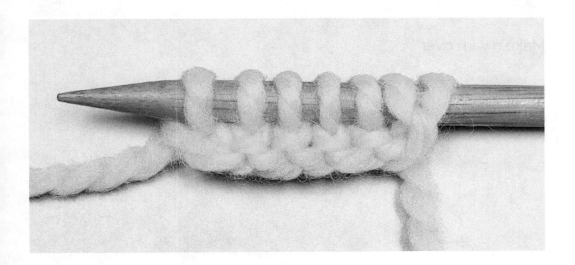

Now, that **the work is properly set up**, we can move to the pattern row.

PATTERN ROW

This is the row that we will **repeat in every row** as we work on our project. It is the same for right-side and wrong-side rows, and it is comprised of two simple steps that we should do in addition to the instructions provided in the pattern we follow.

STEP 1

Bring the working yarn to the front of the work and **slip the first stitch purlwise** from the left needle to the right needle.

Make a yarn over.

To streamline this step, push the tip of the right needle a bit further when you insert it into the first stitch.

This way, the working yarn will lie on the right needle and **the yarn over will be created automatically** when you slip the stitch with the strand of the yarn off the left needle.

Once you finish this step, continue to work according to your pattern, but **stop when you get to the last two stitches** – the yarn over that we made in the previous row + the last stitch. It will be time for the second step of creating brioche selvedges.

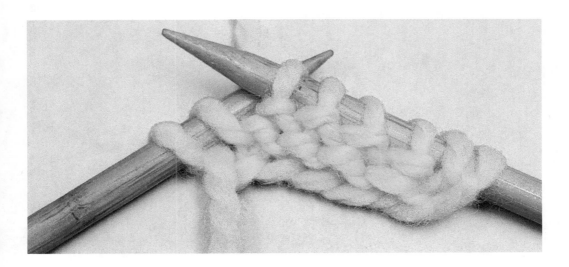

STEP 2

Knit the yarn over and the last stitch together.

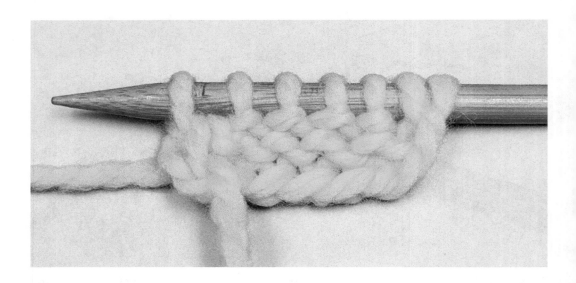

That's how simple it is. **Repeat the pattern row in every row** and watch the side edges of your project become almost three-dimensional.

I've tested this border with stockinette, garter, seed stitch and ribbing, and it looks great with all these stitch patterns. It means that, most likely, this border will work well with the majority of stitch patterns.

SLIM I-CORD EDGING

When we want to make the side edges of our project nice and tidy, it is almost always a good idea to make i-cord selvedges.

Side edges formed by this simple method are uniform. They look nice on both sides of the work and do not stretch too much. But, they **might look somewhat bulky** on projects that do not require additional decoration in the form of an i-cord.

I faced this problem when I was knitting a jacket for my mom some time ago. The front panel was worked in a gorgeous stitch pattern from the collection of Japanese stitches by Hitomi Shida.

The **regular i-cord edging looked too heavy** next to the intricate patterning of lovely twisted cables, and that heaviness made the pattern itself seem less elegant.

As I was looking for a better way to make side edges that are delicate and look good on both sides (the jacket doesn't have a closure), I came up with a method that I called a **"slim i-cord edging"**.

It is a variation of the regular i-cord edging that is **thinner and more elegant**. It will look great on scarves, blankets, cardigans and any other project with open side edges.

As you see in the photo below, this edging **looks equally good next to various stitch patterns**.

I especially like how slim i-cord looks on a fabric made in ribbing. I picked this method to finish the sleeves of the Everyday Tee (one of the patterns I published), and I'm very happy with the result.

Now, that we know how helpful this little technique is, **let's see how we can make slim i-cord edging step by step.**

This edging is worked over two stitches at each side of the work. If you plan to use it to decorate both side edges of your project, **add four stitches to the number of stitches you cast on**.

ROW 1

Knit 1 stitch.

Slip 1 stitch purlwise with the yarn at the back of the work.

Then follow the instructions in your pattern or work in a stitch pattern of your choice if it is a project you "whip up" without a pattern. Stop when you get **to the last two stitches** of the row.

Slip 1 stitch purlwise with the **yarn at the back** of the work.

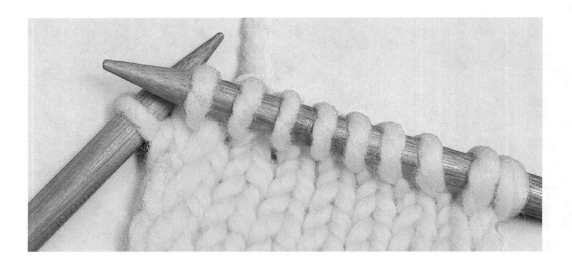

Knit the last stitch.

ROW 2

Bring the yarn to the front of the work and slip the first stitch pulwise.

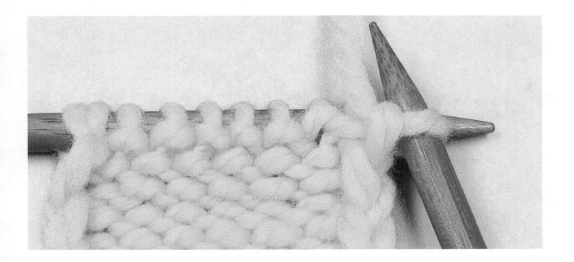

Purl the next stitch.

Work in the main pattern of your project until you get **to the last two stitches** of the row.

Purl 1 stitch.

Slip the last stitch purlwise with the yarn at the front of the work.

Repeat these two rows until your project is finished, and enjoy the amazing well-finished look of the side edges.

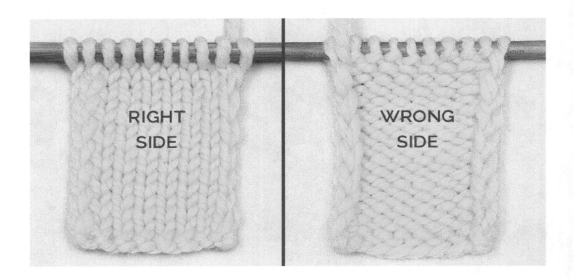

If you find it difficult **to remember what to do when**, keep in mind that **in a right-side row**, we knit the first and the last stitches, and slip the stitches next to them. **In a wrong-side row**, we slip the first and the last stitches, and purl the stitches next to them. That's how simple it is!

In the next section of the book, we'll take a look at **one more way** to decorate the side edges of our projects **with an i-cord**, as well as three other ways to make side edgings **with more than two stitches** at each side of the work.

All you need to do is turn two pages.

Quick reference card

SEED STITCH EDGING

Add **four stitches** to the number of stitches you cast on.

Knit 1 stitch, then purl 1 stitch.

Work in the main stitch pattern to the last two stitches of the row.

Purl 1 stitch, then knit 1 stitch.

Repeat these steps in every row (both right side and wrong side).

Quick reference card

YARN OVER EDGING

Add **four stitches** to the number of stitches you cast on.

RIGHT-SIDE ROW: Make a yarn over, then make a "slip slip knit" decrease.

Work in the main stitch pattern to the last two stitches of the row.

Knit the last two stitches.

WRONG-SIDE ROW: Make a yarn over, then purl 2 stitches together.

Work in the main stitch pattern to the last two stitches of the row.

Purl the last two stitches.

BRIOCHE SELVEDGES

Add **two stitches** to the number of stitches you cast on.

SETUP ROW: Slip 1 stitch purlwise with the yarn in front of the work, then make a yarn over.

Work in the main stitch pattern to the last stitch of the row.

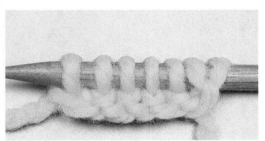

Knit the last stitch.

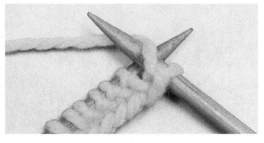

PATTERN ROW: Slip 1 stitch purlwise with the yarn in front of the work, then make a yarn over.

Work in the main stitch pattern to the last two stitches of the row.

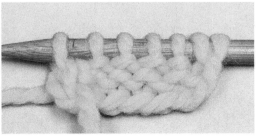

Knit the yarn over and the last stitch together.

SLIM I-CORD EDGING

Add **four stitches** to the number of stitches you cast on.

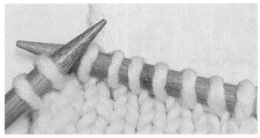

RIGHT-SIDE ROW: Knit 1 stitch, then slip 1 stitch purlwise with the yarn at the back of the work.

Work in the main stitch pattern to the last two stitches of the row.

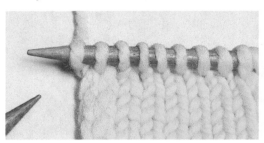

Slip 1 stitch purlwise with the yarn at the back of the work, then knit the last stitch.

WRONG-SIDE ROW: Slip 1 stitch purlwise with the yarn at the front of the work, then purl 1 stitch.

Work in the main stitch pattern to the last two stitches of the row.

Purl 1 stitch, then slip the last stitch purlwise with yarn in front.

MULTIPLE-STITCH EDGES

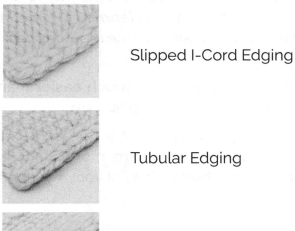

Slipped I-Cord Edging

Tubular Edging

Rolled Edging

Rib Edging

These edges are formed by three or more stitches at each side edge of the fabric.

When using these methods, **check the instructions for each method** to see **how many stitches you should add** to the number of stitches you cast on.

SLIPPED I-CORD EDGING

We'll start this section with a very simple way to add a beautiful i-cord to the side edges of any project. I learned this method from Tom M who kindly shared this technique with me in a comment on one of my video tutorials.

Tom's version of i-cord edging is **much easier** than the regular i-cord edging and the slim i-cord edging (page 47).

It is by far **the easiest way** to treat a side edge with a knit-as-you-go i-cord that I've ever tried. And I'm more than happy to **share this amazingly simple method** with all of you, my friends.

This edging is worked over **three stitches**. If you plan to add it to **both sides of your project** (for example, a scarf or a blanket), **add six stitches** to the number of stitches you cast on.

Then work **the same three steps** in every row.

STEP 1

Knit the first 3 stitches – not together, but **stitch by stitch.**

After the first row, this step feels **a bit unusual** because the **yarn is not attached** to the first stitch.

Ignore this oddity, and **wrap the yarn** around the tip of the right needle **as you usually do** when you knit a stitch.

There is **no need to pull the yarn tighter** after you knit the first stitch.

After you finish a few rows, **pull the edging sideways** (away from the main fabric) and then **pull it down.** You will see that this little bit of extra yarn disappears.

It happens because the **yarn redistributes** between stitches of the edge making them longer and ensuring that the **edging is not too tight.**

STEP 2

Work in a stitch pattern of your choice **until you get to the last three stitches.**

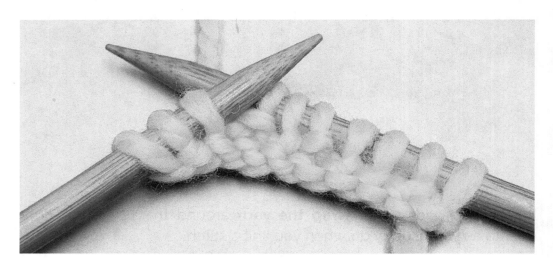

To show off this lovely edging, I'm using **seed stitch** (called moss stitch in the UK) in my swatch. It is more textured than stockinette and **provides a better contrast** to the sleekness of the i-cord.

STEP 3

Slip the last three stitches **purlwise** with the **yarn in front** of the work.

To do that, bring the yarn to the front of the work, then insert the tip of the right needle **from right to left** into the last three stitches (together or one by one) and take the left needle out of those stitches leaving them on the right needle.

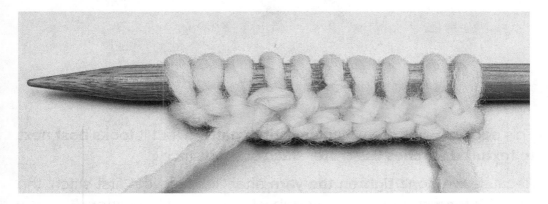

That's how simple it is. **Repeat these steps in every row** and the side edges of your project will turn into **beautiful i-cords** that **look exactly the same** on both sides of the fabric.

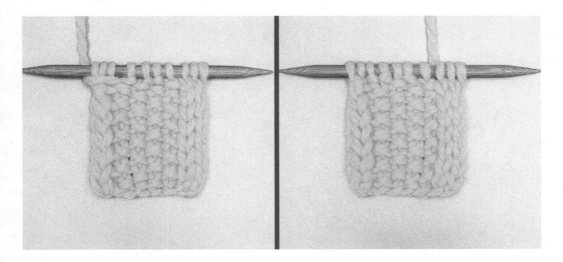

When it is time **to bind off stitches**, bind off the first three stitches as **knits,** and the last three stitches as **purls**.

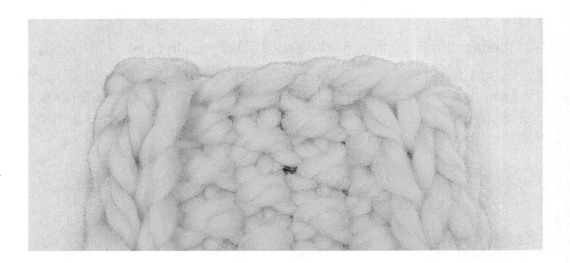

This edging works great with **any stitch pattern**, but it **looks best next to textured stitches** like garter stitch or seed stitch.

Because **we don't tighten the yarn** after knitting the first stitch, the **i-cord is long enough** to comfortably frame any stitch pattern.

TUBULAR EDGING

If you like the look of an i-cord edging, but want it to be flatter, tubular edging is a perfect option to try.

This edging forms lavish edges that **look the same on both sides** of the fabric, and **work great with most stitch patterns**. They are perfect for finishing scarves, shawls, blankets and cardigans.

The fabric formed by the tubular edging does not only look great, it also **stabilizes the edges** keeping them from stretching, and to some extent, even **keeping the edges** of stockinette-stitch-based patterns **from curling.**

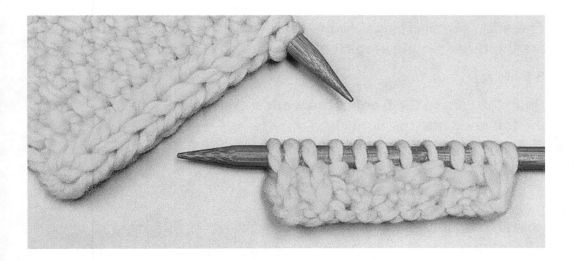

Edges like these ones are the reason why carefully made designer items **look more elegant** than cheap mass-produced garments, even though we can't tell for sure what exactly improves the look of a project.

Let's see how we can **add this gorgeous edging to our knits** in three simple steps.

SETUP

This edging is worked over **three stitches at each side** of the work. If you want to add it to both sides of your project, **add six extra stitches** to the number of stitches you cast on.

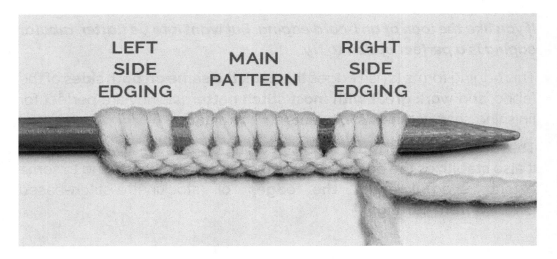

The edge-forming steps are the **same in every row** of the project. They are the **three simple steps** that we will repeat in each and every row.

STEP 1

Bring the yarn **to the front of the work** and slip one stitch purlwise from the left needle to the right needle.

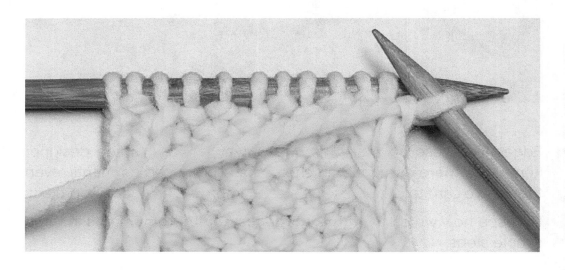

Knit one stitch.

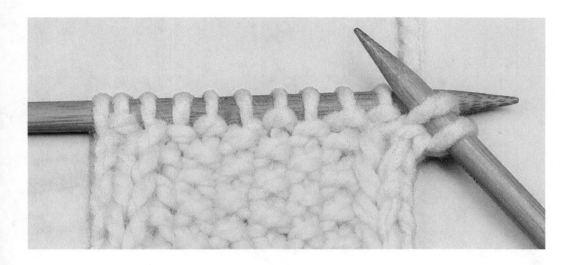

Bring the yarn **to the front of the work** one more time, and slip the next stitch purlwise to the right needle.

These three stitches form **one of the edges**.

STEP 2

Work in **any stitch pattern** until you get **to the last three stitches** of the row.

STEP 3

Knit one stitch.

Bring the yarn **to the front of the work,** and slip one stitch to the right needle. Do it **purlwise,** without twisting the stitch.

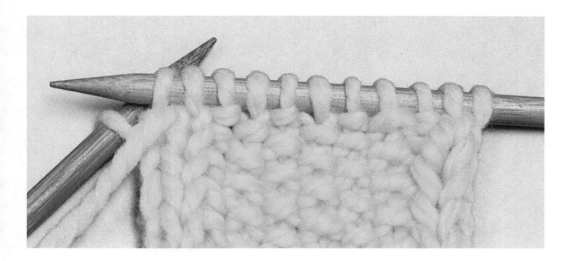

Knit the last stitch of the row.

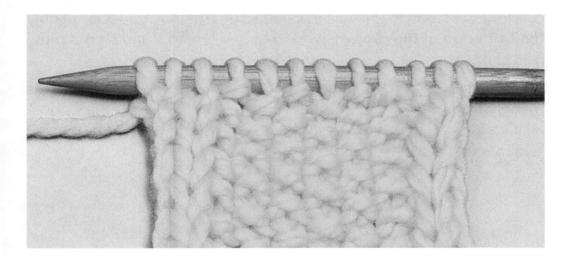

As you see, in the third step we do the **opposite of what we did in the first step** – instead of "slip 1 with yarn in front, knit 1, slip 1 with yarn in front", we "knit 1, slip 1 with yarn in front, knit 1". This takes care of **the other edge** of the fabric.

Repeat these three steps **in every row,** and you will form a beautiful tubular edging at each side edge of your project.

To add this edging **only to the right edge** of the fabric, work step 1 in one row and step 3 in the next row. To use this method to decorate **only the left edge of the project**, work step 3 in one row and step 1 in the next row.

Because we alternate slipping and knitting stitches, the **edging is made of double knitted fabric,** like the one formed by the double knitting technique. That's why the edge is so luscious, and that's why it is **identical on both sides** of the work.

ROLLED EDGING

Quite often, we want the edges of a stockinette stitch fabric to stay flat instead of rolling up as they usually do. But sometimes, the rolled edge can add an interesting touch to a project. The trick here is to control the curling so that the edge doesn't roll all the way to the centre of the project.

The rolled edging method **does just that**.

This edging is a **variation of the i-cord edging**. Unlike the edges formed by the slim i-cord edging (page 47) and the slipped i-cord edging (page 60), the rolled edging is **attached to the fabric only at one side**.

It looks like an **open i-cord**, forming a lovely roll at each side of the fabric, as if the stockinette stitch started to curl in, but then stopped.

What made it stop? **Slipped stitches** that we put between our knits and purls.

We can add these little bits of rolled fabric to the sides of **any project** when we **add eight stitches** to the number of stitches we cast on (four stitches at each side edge of the fabric), and then **work two simple rows** over and over again.

To help you remember to treat four edge stitches at each side edge of the work as selvedges, **separate them from the main fabric with stitch markers**. This will **save you from undoing your work** later on if you accidentally work the edge stitches in the main pattern.

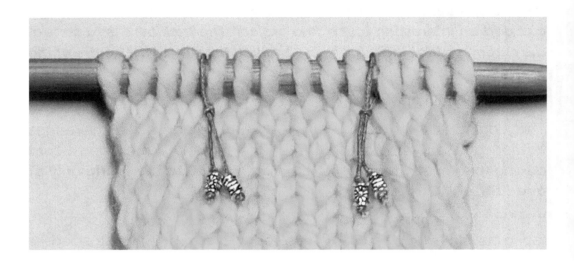

RIGHT-SIDE ROW

[Slip 1 stitch with the yarn at the back of the work, knit 1 stitch].

Repeat the instructions in the brackets **one more time.**

Work in the main pattern **to the last four stitches** of the row (the stitch marker will tell you when to stop).

[Slip 1 stitch with the yarn at the back of the work, knit 1 stitch], work the instructions in the brackets **twice**.

WRONG-SIDE ROW

[Slip 1 stitch with the yarn at the front of the work, purl 1 stitch], work the instructions in the brackets **twice**.

Work in the main pattern **to the last four stitches.**

[Slip 1 stitch with the yarn at the front of the work, purl 1 stitch], work the instructions in the brackets **twice.**

Repeat these two rows as you work on your project, and you will see that the sides of the fabric **delicately roll in** towards the reverse stockinette side of the fabric.

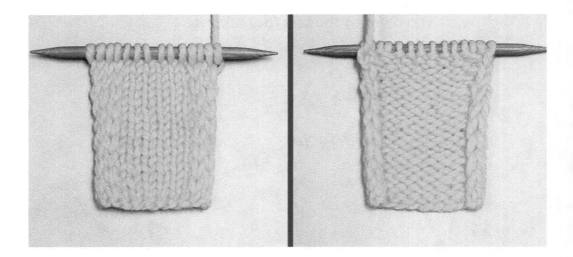

If you want the sides to roll **towards the right side of the project**, work row 1 on the wrong side of the work and row 2 on its right side.

To **make the edging wider,** add an extra **multiple of two stitches** to each side edge of your project, and then repeat the **instructions in the brackets one more time** for each multiple you add.

RIB EDGING

This collection of edgings wouldn't be complete if we haven't added an edging based on ribbing – arguably the most common stitch pattern used to make edgings.

Unlike the rib edgings formed by picking up stitches from the edge of the fabric, the method we are going to discuss in this chapter is **worked at the same time** as the main fabric of the project.

To make sure the very edge of the fabric is neatly finished **without uneven purl bumps** that usually appear at the edge of ribbing patterns, we'll apply **elements of the tubular edging** (page 65) before we work the classic "knit 1, purl 1" sequence.

Through experimentation, I discovered that the **optimal width** of rib edging is **five stitches**. This amount of ribbing is enough to **keep the edge** of the main fabric **from curling**, but it is not too much to overwhelm the overall look of the project.

To add this edging to both sides of your project, cast on **ten extra stitches** (five for each side).

Just as we did when we made rolled edging in the previous chapter, **place markers** between the stitches of the edging and the stitches of the main fabric. This step is **optional, but helpful**.

ROW 1

Knit 1 stitch, and slip the next stitch with the **yarn at the back** of the work. Do it **purlwise**, without twisting the stitch.

Work the next three stitches **in the ribbing pattern** – purl 1, knit 1, purl 1.

Work as instructed in the pattern you follow until you get **to the last five stitches** of the row.

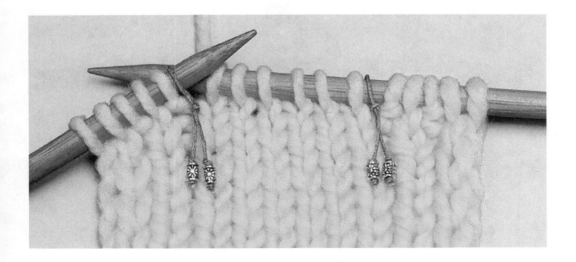

Switch to the **rib pattern** again – purl 1, knit 1, purl 1.

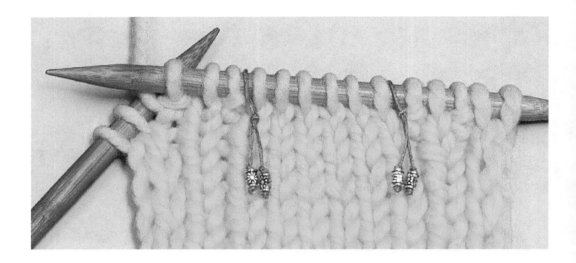

Finish the row by **slipping 1 stitch purlwise** with the **yarn at the back** of the work and **knitting the last stitch**.

ROW 2

Slip the first stitch purlwise with the **yarn at the front** of the work, and purl the next stitch.

Work three stitches in the **ribbing pattern** – knit 1, purl 1, knit 1.

Switch to the main pattern of your project, but stop when you get **to the last five stitches.**

Work in the **ribbing pattern** again – knit 1, purl 1, knit 1.

Finally, **purl 1 stitch** and **slip 1 stitch purlwise** with the **yarn in front** of the work.

Repeat rows 1 and 2 to form neat rib edging that **looks almost the same** on both sides of the fabric.

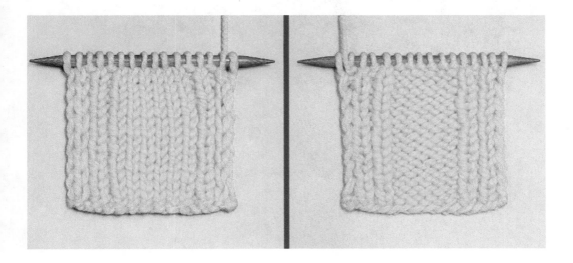

To make the swatch shown in the photo above, I worked **row 1 on the right side** of the work, and **row 2 on the wrong side** of the work.

If you'd like to **reverse the look of the edging,** work row 2 on the right side, and row 1 on the wrong side of the work.

Also, feel free to **make the edging wider**. Simply add one or more multiples of two stitches to each side of your project, and work these stitches in the **same ribbing pattern** as the one we use between the first and the last two stitches and the main fabric.

It is possible to **make this edging narrower** and work it over three stitches at each side of the project. The edging **won't have a distinct ribbing pattern**, but it will keep the edges neat and clean.

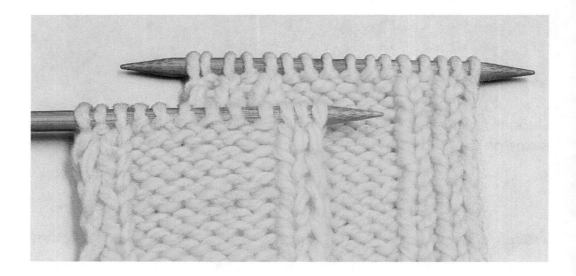

SLIPPED I-CORD EDGING

Add **six stitches** to the number of stitches you cast on.

Knit 3 stitches.

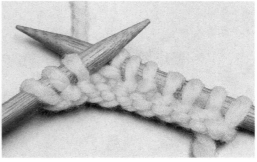

Work in the main stitch pattern to the last three stitches of the row.

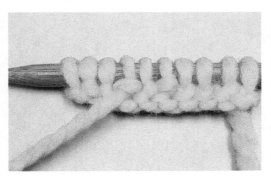

Slip the last 3 stitches purlwise, with the yarn at the front of the work.

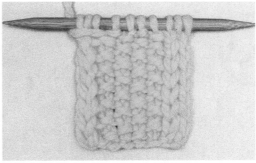

Repeat these steps in every row (both right side and wrong side).

Quick reference card

TUBULAR EDGING

Add **six stitches** to the number of stitches you cast on.

Slip 1 stitch purlwise with the yarn at the front of the work, knit 1, and slip 1 purlwise with the yarn at the front of the work.

Work in the main stitch pattern to the last three stitches of the row.

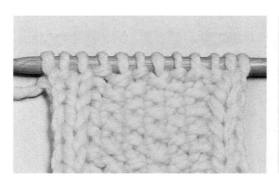

Knit 1 stitch, slip 1 purlwise with the yarn at the front of the work, and knit 1 stitch.

Repeat these steps in every row (both right side and wrong side).

Quick reference card

ROLLED EDGING

Add **eight stitches** to the number of stitches you cast on.

RIGHT-SIDE ROW: [Slip 1 stitch purlwise with the yarn at the back of the work, knit 1]. work the brackets twice.

Work in the main stitch pattern to the last four stitches of the row.

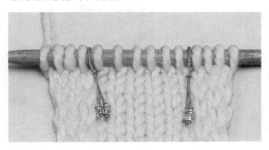

[Slip 1 stitch purlwise with the yarn at the back of the work, knit 1], work the brackets twice.

WRONG-SIDE ROW: [Slip 1 purlwise with the yarn in front, purl 1], work the brackets twice.

Work in the main stitch pattern to the last four stitches of the row.

[Slip 1 purlwise with the yarn in front, purl 1] , work the brackets twice.

Quick reference card

RIB EDGING

Add **ten stitches** to the number of stitches you cast on.

ROW 1: Knit 1 stich, slip 1 purlwise with the yarn at the back of the work, then purl 1, knit 1, purl 1.

Work in the main stitch pattern to the last five stitches of the row.

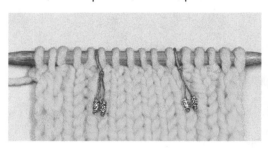

Purl 1, knit 1, purl 1, then slip 1 purlwise with the yarn at the back of the work, and knit the last stitch.

ROW 2: Slip 1 purlwise with the yarn in front, and purl 1 stitch, then knit 1, purl 1, knit 1.

Work in the main stitch pattern to the last five stitches of the row.

Knit 1, purl 1, knit 1, then purl 1 stitch and slip 1 purlwise with the yarn in front.

HELPFUL TECHNIQUES

 Fixing Dropped Edge Stitches in Stockinette Stitch

 Fixing Dropped Edge Stitches in Garter Stitch

 Improving Side Edges After the Project is Finished

 Shaping with Edge Stitches

Now, that we know **twelve ways** to make the side edges of our projects nice and neat, let's see how we can easily **fix dropped edge stitches**, how we can **improve side edges** after a project is finished, and how we can **decrease and increase stitches** without ruining the look of the lovely edges formed by the methods described in this book.

FIXING DROPPED EDGE STITCHES IN STOCKINETTE STITCH

We'll start with the most nerve-racking issue — dropped edge stitches.

Dropped edge stitches are **scary**. If you've ever dropped the first or the last stitches of a row, you know that when the edge stitches unravel, they turn side edges of the project into an **ugly mess** of tangled strands.

The edge looks so messy that it seems that **the only way to fix it is to undo everything** and start from scratch.

Fortunately, the hopelessness of this situation is just an **illusion**. Dropped edge stitches are **fairly easy to fix** when we understand **what's going on** in that scary messy part of our project.

When we drop edge stitches in a project worked in **stockinette or stockinette-based** stitch pattern, we can **easily fix this mess** when we follow three simple steps.

STEP 1

First, we should **catch the runaway stitch** with a pin, a stitch marker or a knitting needle.

Look at the very bottom of the messy part of the side edge and **find the last intact stitch** in that column of stitches.

Secure this stitch with a pin or a stitch marker if you plan to repair the edge later on, or **insert a knitting needle into the stitch** if you plan to do the fixing right away.

When you insert the knitting needle into the last intact stitch, do it **from front to back**.

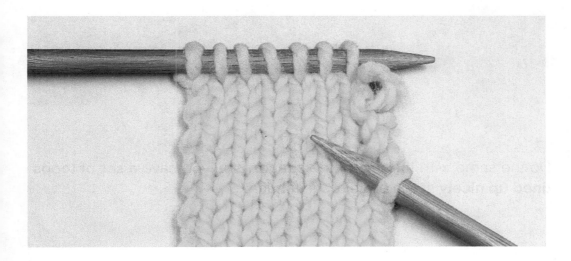

If you temporarily placed this stitch on a pin or a stitch marker, **transfer it to a knitting needle** when you are ready to fix the side edge of your project.

STEP 2

Now, let's **sort out the strands** that form that scary tangled mess above the last intact stitch.

Keep in mind, that the mess is comprised of **a number of loops** – each loop representing the yarn unravelled from **two stitches** – the edge stitch of one row and the edge stitch of the row above.

Carefully **pull the strand at the very top of the edge** to reveal the first loop. If that loop managed to loosen the neighbouring stitches, **tug on it to tighten those loose stitches**.

Do the same with the rest of the strands until you have **a set of loops lined up nicely** at the edge of the fabric.

STEP 3

In this step, we'll **turn each loop into two stitches** the same way as we turn strands into stitches when we **pick up dropped stitches**.

3.1 With the right side of the work facing you, insert the knitting needle that holds the last intact stitch **from back to front** into the loop that is the closest to that stitch.

3.2. Insert the other needle purlwise into that stitch ...

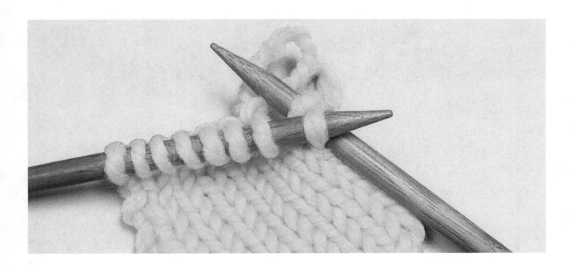

... and pass it over the strand that comes from the loop.

We've just fixed one of the stitches joined by the loop.

3.3. Insert the needle that holds the fixed stitch **from front to back** into the same loop.

3.4. Just as we did in step 3.2, **insert the other needle purlwise into the stitch** and pass it over the strand that comes from the loop.

Now the **loop is turned into two stitches,** and that part of the edge is fixed.

Repeat step 3 until you deal with all loops at the edge of the fabric.

Slip the last fixed stitch **knitwise** to the left needle, and you are ready to **resume working on your project** as if there were no issue with the dropped edge stitch.

If the edge of your project is decorated with **slip-stitch selvedges** (page 10), each loop at the edge will represent **only one edge stitch** that spans across two rows. In this case, **skip steps 3.3 and 3.4** when you fix the edge of your project.

FIXING DROPPED EDGE STITCHES IN GARTER STITCH

We've just discussed a simple way to fix a dropped edge stitch in a project worked in stockinette stitch, or the edge that has slip-stitch selvedges.

Now, let's see how we can fix the **edge of a project worked in garter stitch**, or the one decorated with **garter stitch selvedges**.

Before we get started, let's understand that if we examine one side of a garter stitch fabric, we'll see that **the texture is formed by knit stitches in one row and purl stitches in the next row**. That means that when we pick up a dropped stitch, we should **alternate knitting and purling the unravelled strands** through that runaway stitch.

The **tricky part** here is to decide whether we should start the fixing process with a knit or with a purl. We'll get to solve that mystery **a bit later.**

First, we should **stop the edge stitch from unravelling any further**. As soon as you notice a mischievous stitch sticking out at the bottom of a messy part at the side edge of your project, put a safety pin, a locking stitch marker, a paper clip, a toothpick or anything else you have on hand into that stitch to **make sure it doesn't do any more damage.**

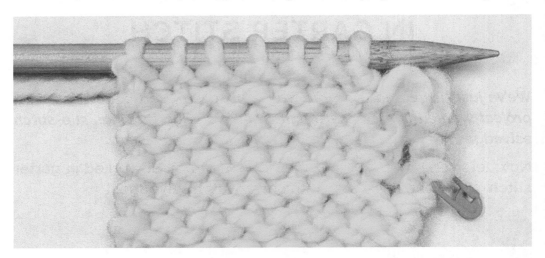

Do it even if you notice this stitch while you are in the middle of a row. **The sooner we secure the stitch, the less mess we'll have to fix.**

Now, let's **sort out the mess** at the edge of the project.

Turn the work so that the unravelled edge is **at the right side of the work**. Hold the messy part with your right hand and **carefully pull it away** from the project.

As you do that, you will notice that what looked like a scary mess is, in fact, **a set of loops**. Not that scary any more, right?

You can also **untangle the loops one by one** starting with the loop at the very top of the messy part of the edge. If a loop managed to loosen the neighbouring stitches, **tug on it** to tighten those loose stitches.

Make sure **all loops** at the edge of your project **are of the same size**.

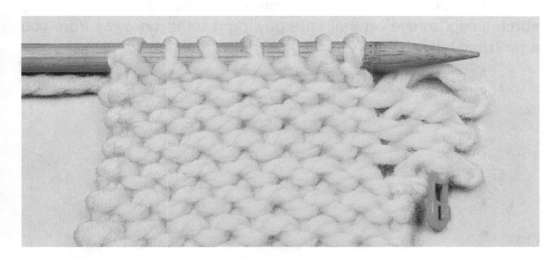

If you have **a half-loop right next to the runaway stitch** (as it is shown in the photo below), take the safety pin out of the stitch, carefully **unravel one more stitch** to release the loop, and put the safety pin back to secure the live stitch.

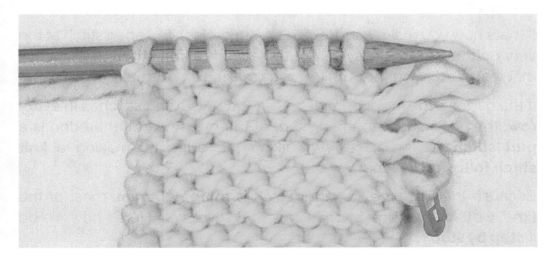

Each loop represents **two stitches** – the edge stitch of one row and the edge stitch of the row above.

We already know that the garter stitch is built by knit stitches in one row and purl stitches in the next row (when we look at one side of a garter stitch fabric), so to fix the edge, **we'll make a knit and a purl stitch out of each loop** we've just recovered.

Place the work on a flat surface, **remove the pin from the runaway stitch** (keep an eye on that little guy, don't let it run away from you again!) and take an empty knitting needle in your right hand.

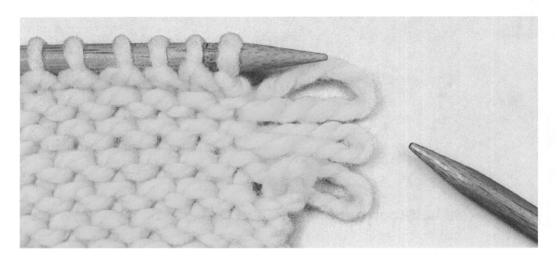

In most cases, the garter stitch is formed by **knitting all stitches in each row.**

If that's how you make garter stitch in your project, the open stitch at the very bottom of the messy part of the edge is **a knit stitch**. That means that we'll start fixing the yarn loops by making a purl stitch.

If the garter edge in your project is formed by **purling stitches in every row**, the **open stitch** at the bottom of the messy part if the edge **is a purl stitch**. In this case, start fixing the edge by making a **knit stitch followed by a purl.**

Because the first type of garter stitch is **more common**, most of the time, we'll fix the edge by making a purl stitch first. Here's how we do it **step by step.**

1. MAKING A PURL STITCH

1.1. Insert the tip of the left needle **from front to back into a loop** that is the closest to the open stitch, and **from back to front into the live stitch** itself.

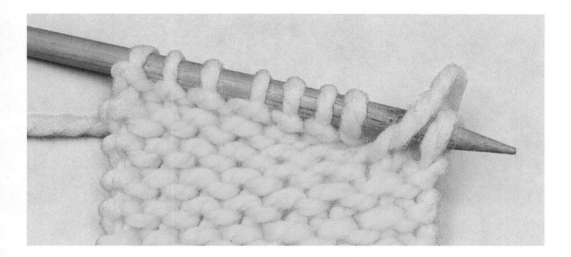

1.2. Use the tip of the right needle or your fingers to **move the loop to the front** of the runaway stitch.

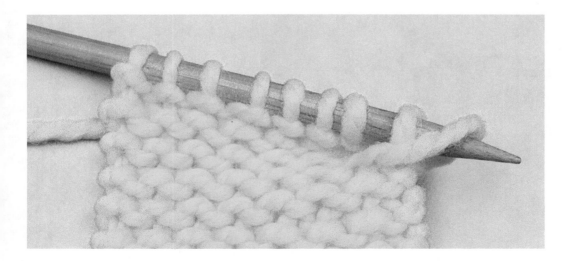

1.3. Insert the right needle **from right to left** into the mischievous stitch.

1.4. Pass this stitch **over the yarn strand** and off the left needle.

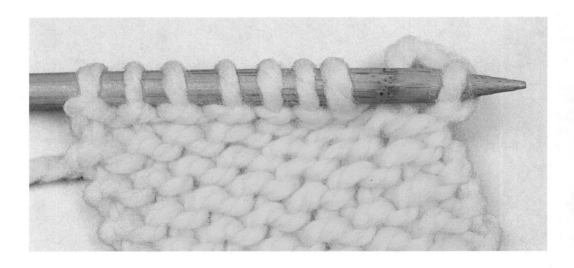

1.5. Slip the resulting stitch **from the left needle to the right needle**. Do it purlwise, meaning that you insert the tip of the right needle into the stitch from right to left, and then take the left needle out leaving the stitch on the right needle.

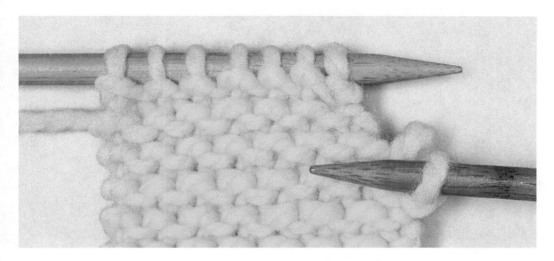

As you see, **we still have half of the yarn loop** hanging behind the fixed stitch. We'll use that loop to **make one more stitch** – this time it will be a knit.

2. MAKING A KNIT STITCH

2.1. With the stitch still on the right needle, insert the tip of the right needle **under the other half of the same yarn loop**.

2.2. Then insert the tip of the left needle **from left to right** into the stitch.

2.3. Pass the stitch **over the strand** on the right needle and off the needle.

We've just turned one of the loops into **two stitches** – a purl and a knit.

Repeat steps 1 and 2 again until you fix all yarn loops at the edge of the fabric.

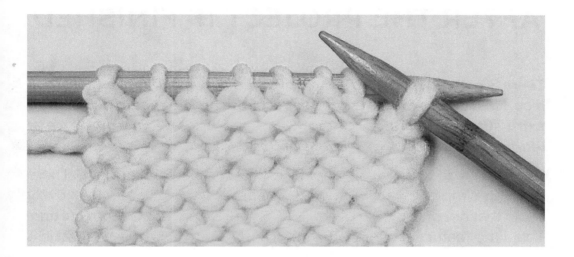

When the edge is fixed, **resume working on your project** as if nothing has ever happened.

The section of the edge that we've just repaired **might be a bit loose**, but you will easily **fix this imperfection** when you block your project.

IMPROVING SIDE EDGES AFTER THE PROJECT IS FINISHED

There is a number of ways to improve side edges and make them look nice. Most of those ways require some planning. We should plan to add extra stitches and remember to work them in a certain way, as we've learned in the first three sections of this book.

But what to do when we want **to fix edges of a finished project**? There is a fairly simple way to turn ugly (let's admit it!) side edges into a lovely chain that not only looks great, but also **keeps the edges from curling**. That little feature is **especially important** if your project is worked in a stockinette, or a stockinette-based stitch pattern.

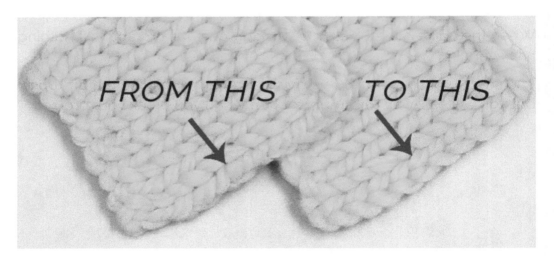

I've learned this tip from an incredibly helpful book **"The Principles of Knitting"** by June Hemmons Hiatt.

It states that we are "*unlikely to find it (this edging) elsewhere*", so we can assume that the author either invented it or discovered it in one of the old knitting books that are not readily available nowadays. In any case, this simple edging **definitely deserves to be known and remembered**.

MATERIALS

This way to make an edging is done with a **crochet hook**. You don't have to be an expert crocheter to make it, but you do need a crochet hook. I find that this technique works best when we use a **crochet hook that is smaller** than the size of the needles we used to make the fabric.

To make the swatch shown in the photos, I used 10 mm (US size 15) knitting needles, and I'll use an 8 mm (L-11) crochet hook to make the edging.

Because we are adding the edging to a finished project, we can make it in any colour we like. For most projects, it makes sense to **use the same yarn that the project is made of**, but if you want to make a decorative edging, use the same yarn but in a different colour.

I'll use yarn in a contrasting colour. Not because I want to make a decorative edge. My reasons are more pragmatic – I simply want to make it easier for you to understand how this method works.

INSTRUCTIONS

Place the project so that **the right side of the work is facing you**. We'll start at the cast on edge and work towards the bind off edge.

EDGING AT THE RIGHT SIDE OF THE PROJECT

STEP 1

Insert the crochet hook from **left to right** under the inner leg of the edge stitch in the first row of the project.

STEP 2

Fold the yarn leaving a small tail, and **place the fold on the crochet hook**.

STEP 3

Pull the yarn through the work.

STEP 4

Now insert the hook **from left to right** under the **inner leg of the edge stitch** in the row above.

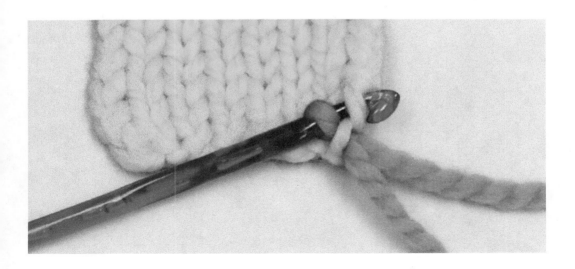

STEP 5

Wrap the head of the crochet hook with the working yarn.

STEP 6

Pull the wrap **through the work and through the loop** that is sitting on the crochet hook.

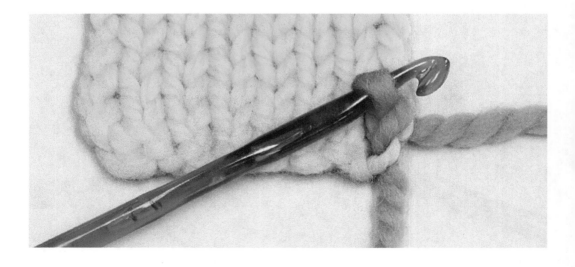

Repeat steps 4, 5 and 6 to work a chain of stitches **along the right edge** of the work.

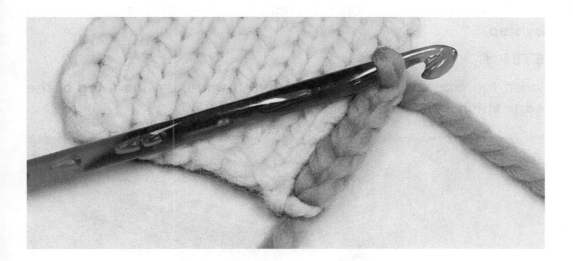

When you get **to the bind off edge**, cut the yarn leaving a small tail (around 10 cm / 4") ,and **pull the last loop out.**

Then weave in both tails.

EDGING AT THE LEFT SIDE OF THE PROJECT

The edging at the left side of the work is done in exactly the same way as the edging at the right side. The **only difference** is that now we'll insert the hook into the work from **right to left**. Here's how we do it **step by step**.

STEP 1

Insert the crochet hook **from right to left** under the **inner leg of the edge stitch** in the first row of the project.

STEP 2

Fold the yarn leaving a small tail, and **place the fold on the crochet hook**.

STEP 3

Pull the yarn through the work.

STEP 4

Insert the hook **from right to left** under the **inner leg** of the edge stitch in the **next row** of the project.

STEP 5

Wrap the head of the crochet hook with the working yarn.

STEP 6

Pull the wrap **through the work and through the loop** that is on the crochet hook.

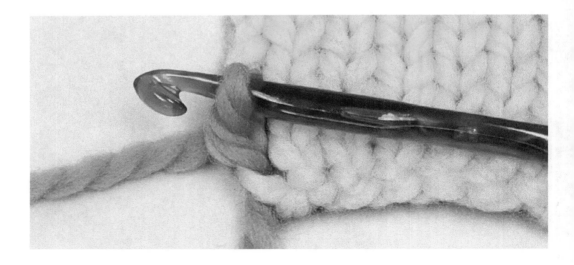

Repeat steps 4, 5 and 6 to work a chain of stitches **along the left edge** of the project.

When you get **to the bind off edge**, cut the yarn leaving a small tail and **pull the last loop** out of the work.

Weave in both tails and enjoy the look of the beautiful edges you've just created.

This edging is **not fully reversible**, though it does **look quite nice on the wrong side** of the work, especially if the edging is done in the same colour as the work.

SHAPING WITH EDGE STITCHES

Necklines, armholes and other shaped parts of our projects look much better when decreases and increases are not placed at the very edge of the fabric. It is especially important when the edges are treated with selvedge stitches or narrow edgings.

But how do we decrease or increase stitches **without ruining the edging**? The answer is simple – we do it **a few stitches away from the edge**.

This method is often called **"fully fashioned shaping",** and we can easily apply it to **any project.** There is only **one limitation** – the fully fashioned shaping is hard to do when we need to decrease or increase **three or more stitches** in the same spot.

Thankfully, most curved parts of our knits have those steep decreases and increases in the **first few rows**. By binding off or casting on several stitches at the beginning of a row, we have to **sacrifice the look of that part of the edging**. It is inevitable, so there is nothing to do but accept this minor imperfection.

The majority of shaping is a **"soft" shaping** with decreases and / or increases made **in every other row.** That's when the fully fashioned shaping method is **very useful.**

The general idea is **very simple** – we decrease or increase stitches according to the shaping instructions in the pattern we follow, but we do it **right after the edging at the right side** of the fabric and **right before the edging at the left side.** Even if the pattern gives very generic instructions, like "decrease one stitch at each side of the work", it is **always a good idea** to do it a few stitches into the main fabric.

How many stitches we should leave between the edges and the line of decreases or increases? **It depends on the project.** If the shaped edges are to be **seamed,** make decreases or increases **one or two stitches away** from the edge. These extra stitches will **not only improve the look** of the project. They will also **make the seaming process easier** and less confusing.

If the edge is **open,** leave as many stitches as you need to make **selvedges or narrow edging.**

Let's **make a swatch** to test this method. Because it is **more common** to do the shaping by decreasing stitches, we'll focus on making **fully fashioned decreases.**

Cast on **10 to 20 stitches** and work a few rows in stockinette stitch or any other stitch pattern you like.

You can **add the selvedges right away** (as I did in my swatch), or do it when we start to make decreases. I treated the edges of my swatch with the **Slim I-Cord Edging** explained on page 47.

Work the **first few stitches in the edging pattern** of your choice. To make the slim i-cord edging, I knitted one stitch and slipped the next stitch purlwise with the yarn at the back of the work.

Now it is time to make the first decrease. To build a **line of left-slanting decreases**, make a **"slip, slip, knit"** decrease.

It is totally fine to use the **classic version** of this decrease, but I prefer a **simplified version**. Here's how it works:

Slip one stitch **knitwise** with the yarn at the back of the work.

Return this stitch to the left needle so that the tip of the right needle is **at the back of the left needle**.

Do not take the right needle out of the stitch. Instead, **push it a bit further** so that it enters the next stitch on the left needle.

Wrap the tip of the right needle with the yarn and pull the wrap through knitting these two stitches **together through the back loop**.

Work until you get to the **stitches of the edging + two stitches**.

The edging in my swatch is worked over two stitches, so I will work in stockinette stitch (the main pattern of my swatch) until I get to the **last four stitches** of this row.

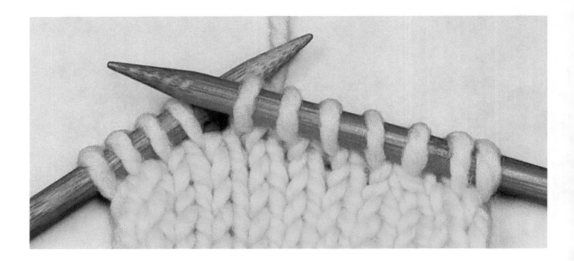

Knit two stitches together to form a **line of right-slanting decreases**.

Then **work the stitches of the edging**.

To make a slim i-cord edging, slip 1 stitch purlwise with the yarn at the back of the work, and knit the last stitch.

If the pattern tells you to decrease **one stitch at each side of the work in every other row**, repeat the steps we've just discussed in every right-side row, and **purl** the stitches resulting from the decreases in every **wrong-side row.**

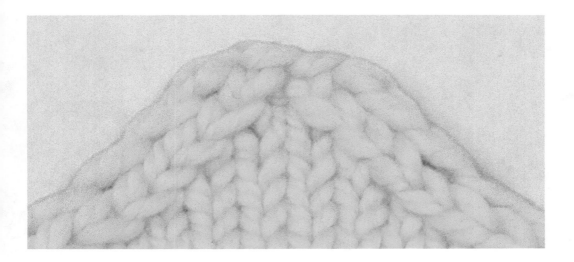

When we need to make steeper decreases and **get rid of two stitches** at each side of the work **in every other row**, we can do it by decreasing **one stitch at each side in every row.**

The right side row will be **the same** as the row we've just worked in our swatch.

In the **wrong-side row**, start by working the **stitches of the edging**. In my swatch, it means slipping 1 stitch with the yarn at the front of the work and purling the next stitch.

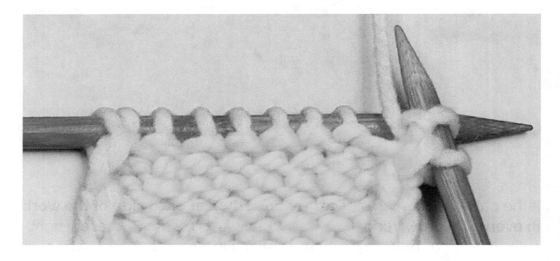

Then **purl 2 stitches together**.

Work until you get **to two stitches before the edging**.

Make a **"slip, slip, purl"** decrease.

First, **slip two stitches separately** from the left needle to the right needle. Keep the **yarn at the front** of the work, and slip the stitches **knitwise** to re-position them on the needle.

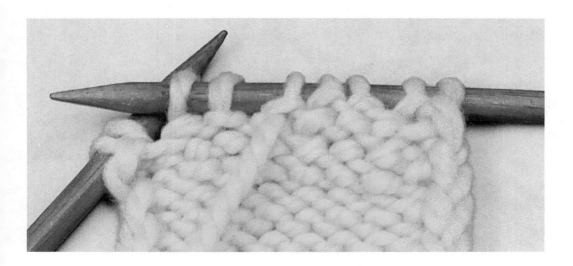

Return the slipped stitches **to the left needle**. This time, we do it **purlwise** without twisting the stitches again.

Purl these stitches **together through the back loop**.

To do that, insert the tip of the right needle into both stitches from left to right **at the back of the work,** wrap the needle with the yarn as you normally do when you purl a stitch, and pull this wrap through both stitches **turning two stitches into one**.

Finally, we are ready to **work the stitches of the edging**. In my swatch, it means purling one stitch and slipping the last stitch of the row purlwise with the yarn at the front of the work.

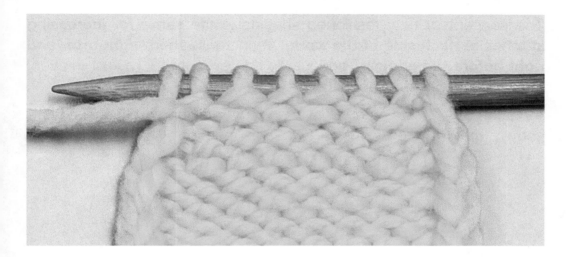

When you make fully fashioned decreases in every row, you will form a **steeper shaping** like the one at the **bottom part of the curve** on the swatch pictured in the photo below.

Note that the **decreasing lines** at each side of the fabric **stay nice and neat** whether we make decreases in every row or in every other one.

These decreases are worked the same way **regardless of the main stitch pattern of your project** if you want to form decreasing lines that look like lovely chains of stitches.

The concept of fully fashioned shaping is the **same for increasing stitches at each side of the work**. We increase them **right after and right before the edgings,** and we do it in every other row, or in every row for a steeper shaping.

As to the way to add a new stitch, use **any method you like**. The well-known **"make 1"** increase usually does a good job.

WAYS TO USE THIS BOOK IN KNITTING GROUPS

One of the ways to learn together with your knitting friends is to run a "learning marathon" by tackling one of the techniques described in this book at each meeting of your knitting group.

If your group meets once a month, by the end of the year you will have a long swatch showing twelve different edgings.

This swatch will come in handy when you choose edgings for your future projects.

If the knitters in your group are more active and meet every week, you will test twelve ways to make neat side edges in less than three months, and you'll have a skinny, scarf-looking swatch as a visual reminder of every edging.

Knitters who get together to make scarves and blankets for charity could try a different approach — use the same scarf or blanket pattern, but let every knitter choose a different edging for their project.

This way, you will see how the choice of edging affects the look of the project. Plus, you will have a great time discussing different edgings and sharing tips.

No matter how you choose to use this book in your knitting group or other knitting gatherings, I hope you and your friends will enjoy learning new knitting tricks together.

Happy knitting!

Maryna

There are more
knitting methods
to explore at
www.10rowsaday.com

CPSIA information can be obtained
at www.ICGtesting.com
Printed in the USA
BVHW011817261122
652777BV00031B/189